# SUMMER HUNGER

Design, layout, cover design: Tania Baban-Natal, Conflux Press

Cover Art: Elliot Elgart

Author photograph: David Meltzer

ISBN 13:  978-1-893670-54-9
ISBN 10:  1-893670-54-6

Library of Congress Control Number:  2010933830

A Tebot Bach book

Tebot Bach, Welsh for little teapot, is A Nonprofit Public Benefit Corporation which sponsors workshops, forums, lectures, and publications. Tebot Bach books are distributed by Small Press Distribution, Armadillo and Ingram.

The Tebot Bach Mission: advancing literacy, strengthening community, and transforming life experiences with the power of poetry through readings, workshops, and publications.

This book is made possible by a grant from The San Diego Foundation Steven R. and Lera B. Smith Fund at the recommendation of Lera Smith.

**www.tebotbach.org**

# SUMMER HUNGER

POEMS

## JUDITH PACHT

**TEBOT BACH • HUNTINGTON BEACH • CALIFORNIA • 2010**

**ACKNOWLEDGMENTS:**

My profound thanks to David St. John, Dorothy Barresi and Richard Garcia for their generous consideration and suggestions, and as before, I'm immensely grateful to my workshop partners. Every poem, maybe every word in the book, has profited from their perceptive give and take.

Special thanks to Leah and Kevin Maines (Finishing Line Press) for permission to reprint *St. Louis Suite*; to the Fort Worth Star-Telegram for permission to reprint excerpts from Gaile Robinson's December 1, 2007 article *(Art-loving Nun is Moved by Early Christian Exhibit)*; and to the following journals and anthologies in which recent poems have appeared: *Chaparrel; Cider Press Review; Georgia Poetry Society Anthology; Los Angeles Review; Margaret Reid Prize Awards, Sailing in the Mists of Time Anthology; Phoebe, A Journal of Literature and Art; Ploughshares; Poems in Memory of James Wright, From the Other World; Poets Against the War; Robert Frost Foundation; Robinson Jeffers Tor House Prize for Poetry; Runes; Site of the City, Los Angeles Postcard Competition; SOLO 6; Spillway Review; Sprout Graphic Press, Invisible Plane, Collected Poems to and about Saints, Angels and Deities; Tebot Bach, An Anthology of California Poets* and *Writers at Work*.

*to my children*

# TABLE OF CONTENTS

*Epigraph*


*Peche Merle*


*Listen history,*
*a hand print found*
*washes time away.*

*Your voice,*
*the sound you uttered*
*pressing palm*
*fingers to stone*
*talks to me of arms*
*like my own.*

*Say you know my warmth*
*and mean to greet*
*your child whose hand fits yours,*
*who hears you speak.*

# WATERVILLE, MAINE, NEAR GREAT POND

There were woods, there were winters, summers and a girl
lying under the elm. She was ten, a new watch on her wrist.
This was enough, this was everything.
She lay on peat from fallen leaves, her cushion of ten times ten.

She was lying under the elm, a new watch on her wrist
the scent of resin and damp earth, musk and bark in the air,
her cushion of ten times ten from fallen leaves
thick and brown from years of slow-melting snow.

The scent of resin and damp earth, musk and bark hung in the air.
That day sun licked the elm leaves, licked her eyelids
as she lay on powdered leaves, thick from slow-melting snow.
A gentle wind stirred the air soft over shallows on Great Pond.

That day sun licked the elm leaves, licked her eyelids —
though something she couldn't reach flickered by.
Wind stirred the air soft over shallows on Great Pond
where she always swam, right over there.

Something she couldn't reach flickered by
and she thought of the sun pressing early spring to summer,
warming where she swam — right over there
where the lazy traffic of birds, a breeze, shook the elm.

*As though the sun is pressing early spring to summer, she thought.*
*This is enough: the breeze, the elm, the lazy traffic of birds.*
There were woods, there were winters, summers in those days.
She set her new watch to keep that time. She was ten that day.

# THE CORE BALANCE TRAINER

touches your hard-to-reach center,
subdues the imbalance that rises
from the belly some days, ballast
for those moods that weigh & shift, those lurches,
though there are times
when even the non-skid tread deep inside

skids,

oblique as abdominal muscles,
your core balance slips away,
pitching and yawing
like the boom
of a gaff-rigged schooner
coming about in an uncertain wind.

as seen in a Hammacher Schlemmer Catalog

## SIDEWINDER

I walk the Albuquerque Road
wherever I am.

Wetlands fool you for a while
but the desert wind rises reckless in clear blasts,
stops you dead in its tracks.

       Today the sand is wind-whipped,
       blows, quiets itself, lies rippling
head low as a snake half-hidden,

though he is here — the lip
that yesterday seemed
safe enough, today snaps

tight as a sewn seam,
hollow tooth hidden under his skin,
the J mark-bruise on mine spells

Judith. Right here. From the rim
of his blue eye
a dark cheek-stripe skims

to his mouth, and I'm
struck, blindsided.
To think I'd given him

my life, my own
and for all those years a home.

Ask, Do we have a plan for Thursday night,
or, What about the biopsy?

To the tongue of the blind, ask means provoke.
Yes. I used to think that was love.

# A JEW IN THE CUPBOARD

*for Tadeusz Rozewicz*

The weather is uncertain out
and inside too as in Poland
after the war.

We talk of Rozewicz renaming
his world: This is a tree, a goat.
This is the rebirth

of spring, a leaf, a man
a woman, whole
after the winter.

Right here drivers move through
an underpass, avert their eyes
to avoid men sleeping,

look away from women
shadowed in doorways.
One, nose bleeding hard,

runs to a doctor. A Walk-in,
the nurse calls out. An Ankle's on the phone
but we don't do ankles here either.

Rozewicz might say
This is a shoe, a bar of soap,
This is a ring, a suitcase.

Ask, What would you do
if threatened? Would you
point to the Jew in the cupboard?

A man, a woman small as a dish.
In a closet a person
can stand tall, hiding.

In a cupboard
an object rests. A small Jew
in uncertain weather.

**CINEMATIC IN LOS ANGELES**


I'm fingering figs
at the Farmers Market
by the new pippins.
It's fall.

       again I see Juana on her back
       only yesterday
       her rounded body
       on the ground
       just outside my window
       the broom askew
       on the concrete
       a wet rag nearby
       Juana    face up in repose

Tonight someone's singing
Leo Frank's soliloquy at the Schubert,
lights are dim, a spot illuminates

       an Ambu bag held high
       force-feeding air to chest
       one breast exposed   one breast erased
       the paramedics move
       as choreographed
       they sliced her checkered shirt
       her pink brassiere
       Juana's bare now waist to neck
       their rhythm   hand to hand
       call   response   no wasted word

       brushed concrete
       where she fell
       brushed her daughter's hair
       readying for a wedding
       to a man Juana knew
       was using her   her weeping rag
       her hard-won green card
       & the words:  gravel  concrete
       broom  mastectomy
       a language not her own

I didn't know her then,
a year ago, or really even now.

     got a pulse?

     no pulse
     seconds lost & gained
     a pulse yet?
     no

     her age?
     49

     up-down-in-out
     retracing steps   flashing lights
     siren streaking
     down Wilshire

A scent of fresh air in the sun-dried sheets folded today

     they threw her cut shirt
     over her before speeding away

The plants are fed,
air and water bubble down the coffee filter.

     the thud again
     no groan no cry
     run    go where?
     do what?
     call 911      pick up
     the walk-around phone
     I hear a strange voice
     calm & loud
     the voice is mine

     still air   still body
     Juana flat
     on her back
     her forehead's
     cooling now

no rising chest
only spittle   a gentle drool
almost forgotten
Juana's rubber sandals
float upsidedown
with bits of palm frond
in a puddle

Today they came for her shoes.

# JENIN, PALESTINE, APRIL 2002

Because of what happened here,
because of what did not happen,
the soldiers move from house to house
in the densely peopled camp.
I know that camp. Many things don't
go on as they did, but a few do.

Only a few know what to do
because of what happened here.
Soldiers and the people don't
feed their dogs now. It could happen
again. How many in the camp
used to have a goat, a house,

a place to call their own? Housed
in lean-tos, how many still do?
The scraping of a pot in camp
scatters the pigeons. Over there
a chicken scratches for seeds that happen
to lie around the rubble. *Don't,*

someone said, *Careful, don't
touch anything in the house.*
One remembered what could happen:
walls falling, not knowing what to do
because of the confusion here
and what had swept through the camp.

How many may have stayed in camp
no one knows but those who don't
turn up – well, concrete's here
instead, just rumors where a house
had been. Those who do
turn up sweep, stack. Some happen

to actually hear those buried alive. It happens.
Rumors? Well, they may be true. In camp
either way people do
know who's gone. They don't
listen to officials checking the house
(or whatever's left of it here)
who ask, *What happened?* They don't
answer in the camp, but the houses
only concrete shells, speak here

# THE DEAL


No one pulls her —
She goes willingly,
enjoys the bruises

on her upper arm
under the blue shirt,
reveres his mind,

the smile, the tongue
that reels off history:
Plutarch's *Advice*

*to Married Couples,*
*Constantine's Sword.*
The show of intellect

turns her on, She'll promise
anything when he talks
mean or smart, scares her

on the Autostrade swerving
through a soggy stretch
locals call the Styx.

She lives with hell
and likes it,
his three-headed habits

dropping clothing everywhere,
stacking dirty dishes with the clean,
She won't reveal the third.

Meanwhile
he comes and goes
no questions asked,

which works for her
as long as she can take
the ride—oh, how she loves


the ride—from Vicenza
along the river
to see the villas

of Palladio,
as long as she can
suck the sweet-tart juice

of pomegranate seeds.

**STILL LIFE ON A TABLE TOP**


Let these objects stand for everything:

I know the glass top doubles
the knife. I know two blades pierce.

Your tongue. Two tongues forked
saying *Yes* and *No,*

*No* covering the *Yes.* The knife and fork.
The two white saucers, two cups.

The mirrored dregs of coffee grounds
blurred by layers of light

glancing off the glass. The search
for where the table's hard edge ends

and what's real begins.
Who is your sister,

the one you said you had?
You have no sister, only a brother

whom you never see. You, sightless
as this carved Eskimo's Janusian head,

as his rounded sandstone back,
his four blind hands that give

and take away at one time.

## TWO DOUBLE AGENTS

He slides into the scene
seamlessly, slips the papers
low onto the ledge,

the dead drop spot below the bridge.
Another part of him
has shifted deep inside

the way a well-oiled lock moves silently
tumbler to tumbler. He knows
when to open and close the cylinders,

when to calculate algebraic X & Y
add pi, talk fission, think fusion,
gain entry to both sides.

It's not the fifty-thou
it's the thrill of deception —
a high higher than

the ecstasy he feels singing
*The People That Walked in Darkness*
at Christmas Mass each year,

higher than two shots of single malt on an empty stomach,
a game played on an edge sharp enough
to draw blood.

❊

And she (or call her me) married at nineteen,
old enough to bear a child, living out a role. Faculty wife.
Blinded by the curling smoke, the pipe, the pose.

Books and planks and bricks, the dust-scuffed car
but oh the pride of poverty, and she could cut
a skirt, no pins, no pattern.

Plaid curtains sewn by her own hand,
she'd mastered the meringue, the braise of beef.
Nineteen, Spinoza and the essay finished, but not a scholar,

never that. Lying alone on the rented mattress
she wondered, *Who am I?* not *Who do I want to be?*
Featureless as an unformed fetus,

no pretense, simply adrift,
floating unmasked.
Terrified.

## SURFACE

Like a motel, the table by the bed
the dressers, veneer, everything
matching, serene and restful as motels
are meant to be, for the business traveler
who clinches a merger, the hungry lovers
who clinch and merge,
the invisible room
service, the waiter's smile as he enters
each opened door,

although you know, some days
with an ear to the facing, you can hear
the plywood peeling strip by strip,
the glue melting, dissolving to liquid,
and in a wind the water roils oily black
or turns viscous, even tears the heart,
all the while the veneer's shining smooth,
the grain unmarked,

and who would know, or even care, unless you prized
something solid, something durable, unless you counted on it.

*

*Words wait*



*as a mother bird
pushes her fledgling
to take wing*

*even though
his first steps tremble.
He falls.*

*At noon in sultry
shade or in midnight's
bright moonshadow*

*he eats, she feeds
leafhopper, springtail
beak to beak*

*and one day
he stands steady,
stands*

*seeing
with his focused
jet-bead eyes, inside,*

*stands
remembering steady
and how he got there,*

*he stands
for all that's beating
under his feathers.*

*On a good day
he flies off the page.*

# SMALL THINGS

Red clay tradebeads in a dreadlock braid,
the scent of earth-musk after rain,
a cicada chorale shrieking in the sun,
the summer's chalky grass, oak-black shade.
Praise the sticky pollen on the bee's
hind legs, the blossom's private parts, the fruit.
Praise all vowels: *masa* and *metate,*
*smooth* and *avocado, quesadilla.*
Praise Nomo backing first base on Beltre's throw,
Cohen reaching Ahmed, Ahmed reaching
words both used to know, speaking, speaking.
Praise the wild geese rising slow,
circling after rain to taste the scent
of air, of earth, this earth.

# SPINACH

Sweeping across the plain
flat as far as anyone can see,
wet beating wet,
the memory, the after-rain, the earth,
this touch of wild perfume
from field to city sink.

Rain's forgotten as I cook,
adjust the flavors, heat, grind peppercorns,
melt butter into leaf to garlic-seep.
Three squalls ago last week just days apart
the spinach leaves bent double,
picked in sun, packed into quarts,
collapsed to cups, to pan, the liquid sapped.
And here, limpid greens
arranged as art on porcelain.

This morning I thought, *Spinach for tonight,*
and so passed up some carrots picked too soon,
designer beets and tasteless apples
paraffined for shine.
But the collard greens looked full
loosely tied with twine,
and zucchini flowers bloomed.

# BACKYARD

Spring and spiders couple, bud and leg
or, more precisely, insects lay their eggs
in woodpiles, on the underside of orange tree
leaves—the yard's a hatchery.
Vines splayed along stucco sprout and turn,
a pile of loam and logs seethes mealy worms,
a hundred greens, some gray, some silver sage,
sprout loud. The air rubs soft, the blue jays rage.
Well, I for one watch the year unfold
through windows from inside, my desk chair rolls
from phone to one more crossed out scrawl.
The pen. Another line or two—then, *Stall,*
I tell myself, a voyeur taking time
to ogle spring, set eggs and legs to rhyme.

**WEATHER**
three bouts-rimes


This is the month air spits out June,
pretty June of the freight train's roar, of stress
churning funnel-like—June of the placid moon
staring blank-faced down inside. Winds obsess,
weave in and out. Think of a basket, snake
on snake, a nest of vipers writhing. Moot,
the celebration of who lives—cake
is icing, taste is life itself. *A beaut,*
the sucked up voice vanishes like a Garbo
smile, like the Listener in Beckett's play.
Air twists the wrung-out rags of clouds, takes a hobo,
takes the nursing infant's mother. Gone, as day
turns coal, as Death taunts, shakes his rhinestone
scepters, reeks of grim cologne.

✳


But something's turned on edge—just see what June
inflicts on hot July, expectation? Stress?
No—though something steals the August moon.
The hour's dusk and we obsess
again on what to eat, coil snake-
enjambed, limb on limb. Dessert is moot
now that we're filled, devouring (cake-
like) each other. I read your skin, read beaut
as beaut-iful, the aftertaste of sweet. Garbo
can have *Alone, Alone,* her game, her play.
You, haunches swinging under your hobo
chic, make Sunday every day.
You, facets dancing from a rhinestone,
scent the air with new-mown hay's cologne.

✳


*29*

Yes, for the poet any day in June
will do. A bud's soft green or even stress
can birth a sonnet, say, about the moon,
poor beleaguered over-written moon. Obsess
and write, obsess and write — or snake
through both to dream of blue. Moot
again the swirling winds, bouts-rimes not scanned, no cake-
walk here — but give it time. *Beaut*
I start and cross it out, think of Garbo,
of her mask, her barely smile, play
with exhausted words, tie them as a hobo
ties his clothes with rope. Is this a sonnet day
I wonder, a day to write the yellow rhinestone
white? To wander, slant-rhyme roam, cologne?

# SISTER WENDY AT THE KIMBELL

Last week she stood where I stand now,
near the Reliquary Cross, bejeweled and sunlit,
near tombs in quiet light, her voice hushed.

> *It begins with the semi-shadows of the catacombs*
> *and the scared little people ... ends with this sunburst.*

At the statue of the Good Shepherd

> *Here you have this beautiful, strong young Jesus*
> *caressing that sheep he has lifted and all the other*
> *sheep are waiting for their turn.  I found this*
> *more touching than I can find words to express,*

and the ram's hoofs dig into her own back
as they did the Shepherd's.

At the statuette of Saint Paul

> *so small and plain with a big nose. Oh,*
> *you darling man — but all this is unimportant,*
> *what's filling his heart is so moving.*

❖

               Astonishing,

I, a non-observant Jew, read
the observant's mood, see Wendy as my kin:
we both translate myth to burning flesh,
shiver in another's cold, shrink time.

❖

Some days I'm Daphne changing sheets,
pulling dying gnats from under the ficus tree.
The housework and the housework —
as he begs, *Light my life* (as if I would). I'd
leave the lot for damp earth,
only run and run through laurel.

Some days I'm Persephone
flying down the *Autostrade* with you,
that soggy road locals call the Styx.
Ever since the night you tempted me,
the night you said, *Just this time,*
*just a seed or two,* so I sipped
the pomegranate juice, you know the rest.

Now in the heat deep down when you are gone,
I trace the line along the bony ridge
of your nose to your upper lip. Your brow.
I can even taste the scent of you.

## TO A FOSSIL

*Olduvai Gorge, Tanzania, 1959*


Hide and seek,
a run under palm frond canopies.
After someone like me must have drowsed
on jackal pelts, you rank with sweat,
steaming, four arms, four legs tangled,
listening in the yellow-eyed dark
for the crackle of a step from the streambed
where rivercresses grow.

You slept away millennia
in sediment with hare and fish and bird,
once carrion of the hawk
circling above. Even now
he eyes the rifted gorge. Spies your jaw.
You, blood to stone to hand, my hand
that pulls you from the hot earth,
speechless.

# THE DREAM



I don't love you as if you were salt-rose or topaz,
each one only an imitation of elegance.
The salt-rose petals edge themselves in chalk,
masquerading damask flowers, discreet and pale

as sea air—their ragged blooms look best
at a distance, just like that other dissembler,
topaz. Not amber or diamond, it seems glass
but calls itself yellow sapphire, a pretender

like the rose. No, I love you because you let your hair
go grey, for your humor, raucous or dry,
for warm body nights, cold air, your scent of musk,

your even breaths in sleep, a dream we've told
each other deep and bottomless, one
that's real as life and growing old.

# FARMERS MARKET

(it is Friday)

His doctor scans the blood work:
the IgAs, the IgMs

the absolute neutrophils, the lymphocytes.
A protein spike...

(A sudden rustle of paper in the way
wind kicks

fall leaves, a clicking FAX
as a woodpecker

pierces bark with his beak
to the bare trunk.)

... *But what does it mean,* he wants to know.
The doctor,

placing her face close to his, answers
*Myeloma,*

and when he winces she insists
*Don't you want to know?* —

and yet the blood, the urine, normal.
Another draw,

another vein, another week
to wait

as inside his bone marrow he knows
tumors grow,

wonders how fatigue & pain slide into death.
Dark chard

clumps, pools of heirloom tomatoes
knarled and whorly, breed

for generations, beans and fertile eggs,
burst their shells,

live, shrivel, die.
Today it is Friday a week,

the test results are due.
Lemons

rest mounded as always in the stall
tempting,

luminous, lit from within
by early sun.

Lemons to juice, to squeeze or freeze
in cubes for the future.

*Shall I buy them?*
He passes the mound.

*

The call: *Normal
on all counts* —
why not lemons, then?
The zest,

translucent shavings of peel
fragrant

with oil – they perfume the thumb
and forefinger

and of course
he buys them, twelve.

One fat dozen. Not for their flesh
or seeds,

but for tomorrow's juice.

❋

*Bird*

A slice of sheep cheese with apple…

*you were saying*
*when the window shook*

*—or was it the whole wall—*
*and on the ground a wren,*

*beak and needle talons*
*in barest motion,*

*obsidian eyes*
*dazed, fooled by light*

*seeming air, seeming*
*endless as sky.*

*Who hasn't flown*
*too fast and high,*

*song full*
*in the belly*

*sun-warm after a rain,*
*the sweet taste*

*dazzling. Sometimes*
*it ends this way,*

*a blind fracture*
*after a moment*

*of so much*
*so complete,*

*that fullness under*
*wild-streaked feathers.*

Feel her, she's still warm.

## TOXIC

A terrible beauty was born and slept —
well, feigned sleep through an endless
night, crouching brilliant and black,
hungering deep inside your marrow.
Today it leaps, exciting cells, the white
and white and white.
We walk the halls, you, me, our chrome-plated
friend, four-legged on wheels, swinging
plastic bags as if they were hair,
clear fluid sloshing with every step,
tubes dripping a potion into your veins:
10 ccs for 4 hours, 30 ccs for 10 minutes.
Will *Idarubicin, Vincristine,* stop it dead
—or does it hide   waiting?

# LUCANUS CERVUS



*Are you the widow?*
the man asks her
in Social Security prose.

She is hidden deep inside,
far from the sounds
even a conch remembers
from the salt sand,
her beetle claws pluck
with pincher teeth,
her armor
a three-segment carapace.
Even strewn with widow-
weeds her shell is black.

She says, *No,*
*I am Lucanus cervus —*
*can you hear me from deep inside?*
*His number was 208 34 6637.*

## AFTER RAIN

We could have scattered Jerry's ashes earlier
at Con's cottage, but in the morning a slide
blocked the highway, besides I thought
the creek too wide and fast to cross,
the shifting clouds uncertain, the downhill
still too slippery for Robert since his stroke.
Indian Paint Brush might have flowered in time
with heat and light—another reason to delay.

On Sunday Robert said, *We can do it,
the breeze is blowing the clouds away.*
The plastic box lay in Jerry's study
six feet from where he sat for twenty years
at his desk under the lamp that mimicked daylight,
the one he wouldn't use. Jonathan carried the ashes
from the shelf out the door. We said it at one time:
*Jerry's last trip across the back step.*

From the top of Solstice Canyon the ocean shone
the clear blue-black of after rain, the green spring hills
cut steep to the sea. We snaked downhill to the creek
on the leaf-slick trail, forded the stream hopping stone to stone,
shouted above the roar to warn each other of a loose rock.
John Mottishaw's legs planted, two solid trunks set mid-stream
to steady us, water lapping his hipboots.
Last of all he carried Robert across on his back.

Just above us, Con's cottage or its stone ruins—
where Jerry wanted to be. No one got speechy,
only Elliot told a joke in honor of the Master Joke Teller
and we slurped orange and grapefruit segments
for all the citrus Jerry loved but couldn't eat.
Jonathan opened the plastic box
while we watched wind dust the air, the laurel leaves,
ourselves, all silver with scattered ash.

# HORROR VACUI

Howling high-pitched yips last night,
a dog set off another down the block
back and forth, insistent and incessant,

breaking sleep wide open. Say it was footsteps,
hunger for a touch, or food,
or the calm that comes from filling

quiet with a voice. Or an elegy of sound
instead of sight, like covering every wall
and table top with floral leaves and bric-a-brac.

But that's the point, there's a kind of solace
some would say who feast on patterns everywhere,
fearing empty space.

I've done it too, talked of nothing on the phone,
moved to rooms with choruses on tape
to keep from thinking,

measured sound and silence,
straining for the slide of slippered feet
on mourning floors. I've eaten when I'm full

to fill what won't be filled.

## RAIL COLLISION, ATWATER VILLAGE
## JANUARY 26, 2005, 6 AM


sliding gravel   wind shear
    but no wind
                nothing
an open
    briefcase   two men flung
to the floor   moving
        entrails
  of smoke

❉


an arc of sparks     the car
rockets   the screech of ripping metal

    black soaks the air
flame splashes her skin

    and there's no path
to the falling light

❉


    just dozing   before the jolt

❉

dust
  tables flying     the taste
of salt     the char
     of wild roses

           an absence of air
even of pain
    surprising
isn't it     I'd have thought at
least
    flashes     of my lace shawl
 a flicker     something     the photo
  of us in the blue frame
 something     not
even a dream     between
   crash and silence

# ALBUQUERQUE

You wanted to be Mozart but your timing was off.

*Wind gusts may exist*
says the sign on the I-40, they sweep
morning down the blue

striped balloons drifting
past my breakfast
toast. Mesa and bosque rooted low,
a rivernet along the Rio Grande.

Up here wind *gusts may exist,*
up here *It's a Mozart day*
says the voice on the radio.

I dreamt last night of remembering
you in hospital. No, you were not,
but when I went to your room the bed was empty

and more, it was not your bed.
It was someone's, and I was too late,

my timing was off.
I'd not forgotten you, you
who gulped a Mozart day

(today it's cold dry clear). You who

never wanted, and for good reason,
this place, the altitude, that's now mine.
Well I have it and once more

my timing's off.

# A VIOLENCE OF SEASON

Cold drops like a hawk
on Blue Hill, Maine.
It bores into the skin, the heart,
claws the eye.

She craves and fears
the imprint of weather:
piles of leaves waiting
for a ceremony of scented smoke,
the shrinking day, the sun's
oblique afterthought, cool on rooftops.
The stubbled field. A lace of frost.

She longs for rain to freeze,
to blow dark and sideways,
smack the barn broadside
smack the back, drape the limbs
of staggering trees.

Behind    gray rubs gray     the horizon spare as a pencil line.

*

At last the fat-cheeked bulbs spring shoots.
And then, ear close to the earth,
She hears their damp breath, watches
for the yellow-wild iris to feather,
the birch and oak to bud.

On Narragansett's shore
a fractured moon marks the tides,
tracks the dunes' drifts and hollows.
She hunts clams in the wet sand
where the shallows ebb.
Fingers water-puckered toes
feeling for the quahog's shell
treading fast and deep.

*

She craves and fears the fever of August,
the airless weight of it on the briny pond, the serpentine.
August, the month her daughter rested on her belly,
cord attached—shared blood, shared heat.
This newborn, warm—she still remembers warm.

Her girl, legs long as a filly, temper short,
barefoot in the roundup against the war, barefoot
at the police station, sandals swinging, hair swinging,
broad mouth, broad smile, conscience wide
and deep

gone with summer

in this violence of season,
as cold claws at the eye, shudders,
drops like a hawk.

Jane Siegel
August 8, 1955—August 2, 1972

# THE CLOSING

Call it a mercy, dark from the inside.
She can see it, the opening
and quickly the closing

that holds the numbing close,
keeps the other out —
splashes of sound

shaking light-like
through the pittosporum's
sulky leaves.

> What if I had said
> or you had said,
> *here's money for the trip* or
> why had I not said
> *don't drive that thing*
> or if you had said
> you must have said
> if I had only said
> and can we please
> just one time
> only this time
> can the ride be safe?
> can the plane land
> on the tarmac
> flaps up  wheels down?
>
> Maybe she'll be back.
> I ran after a girl —
> one shoulder hiked high,
> head tilted as though
> listening as is her way,
> hair sun-streaked, swinging
> fast   just a glimpse
> of course it was someone else

or maybe you'll say to him
*wake up! blow liquid silk*
*the way you always do,*
*blow those round notes*

*from your bassoon,*
and he'll wake up
whole    just as he was.

The closing again,
the erasure only
for the sleeping hours

not the abyss
that sucks her in, even though
she holds the outer edge

hangs tight on the lip of it
resisting
fighting the pull

all the while looking into the dark,
the round, swirling, sucking,
insolent
abyss looking smack back
into her heart's eye.

**FALCON**
Dunnsmuir, Scotland


Never mind *diurnal*, I know

you seize the day, calculate
fly-time to the fraction

of a wink, those unblinking

gold-flecked eyes
measure the hare's gait

from half a mile. Wing-swing, dive,

thunderbolt of notched beak
quick to the back, snapping it.

It's what you dream at night I want to know,

how sleep hones precision:
below, the darkened field of oil seed rape

or gorse, the tremble of a stalk,

the twitching ears, the scurry.
You know the carrion's mind or spine,

how to break each one
precisely—a kind of nocturnal

practice for a clean kill
not sport, not

human fantasies
splayed,

hooded black
or red on a concrete floor

like those, say
in Abu Ghraib.

*

*Now:*


*This is not the time.*
*Yesterday's wind is still,*
*desperate for sleep.*

*Sneak in under a dream, strike*
*the unguarded thought*
*in streaming light.*

*Turn, go back*
*and come closer; the book's*
*written, read, reread.*

*Read it back*
*to front as Hebrew*
*but come closer;*

*closer.*
*Move back to front*
*as Hebrew reads*

*when written. Read, reread.*
*Closer, the book says,*
*turn and go back.*

*In streaming light, strike*
*the unguarded thought,*
*sneak in under a dream,*

*inside sleep.*
*Yesterday's wind still thirsts.*
*This is the time.*

## PIECING

Days went by before mother asked
*Where is that silk?*

and I, nesting in her yellow quilt
traced the pieces, counted stitches.

Father brought two satin scarves from France,
one splashed paisleys, purple, gold,

for Mother—yes, the perfect match
for her evening gown, her beaded bag.

For me, the school-girl blue.
Hers matched my iridescent taffeta,

would cling to me as skin, floating
at the senior prom with Roger Rose

as the mirrored globe turned slow, scattering
green and rose confetti-light around, around.

Her open drawer, the scented scarf,
gone without a word

simply slip-streamed in the dark, fluttering
wing-like as silk will do, sliding into moon-leaf shadow.

I tried to say *I borrowed it*
but fingering the quilt threads wondered if

what bound me safe would snap—
if truth was worth the telling.

## SEVENTEEN


when I knew nothing much and everything,
remained silent when I heard
a word like *estrous,* wondering if it might bring

me new personas, tried them, made them disappear
like actors' parts in an imagined play.
Such was recreation. I had no fear,

tried my best to lead someone astray,
instead was led. There was someone —
older of course, I thought him prey,

susceptible — me the courtesan
flashing smiles and a Spinosa book,
the cover prominent, praying that chance,

distraction, or the Lord would save me from a look
that said, *You're faking it,* that he'd not ask
me to defend Monism or Descartes. I took

to rhyming terza rimas, thinking fast
to make the evening's conversation pass.

# SUMMER HUNGER, NEW YORK CITY

Start with the flat roof
where soot crackles under leather soles,
where pigeons peck crusts that wind lifts
over the parapet, necks jerking, faces turning
one way, the other, like windup toys
searching, waiting for their breadcrumb-dream,
as black grit drifts over tarpaper softened
from heat, days of heat pressed into granite,
into skin and skull, past bones to where
the sun scours cool reason away.

We set beach towels end to end,
let the rays toast one side, then the other,
turn our girlish reveries
to the Beauty of the Boyfriend, practice
the fluttering hand, the cinched waist,
imagine the rustle of a patterned skirt
all leaves and roses swaying just so at the hem,
consumed by what might
(it could you know    anytime now)
blow over the parapet.

## WOMAN/CHILD

Overnight it seems her breasts have budded
the way bulbs bulge in early earth —
she inspects her newly profiled chest
in the bathroom mirror every night.
Not long ago she fit with room to spare
inside the kitchen sink. Splashed
I'd get a bath myself then dry her
wet and churning, swaddle her
in a flannel mummy-wrap. I can't believe
she conjugates *jeter*, can flick a sassy kick
at me without a wobble in high heels! She who burst
forth in August like a summer honeydew, overripe
splitting open, lay fleshy-warm on my belly —
now talks of breaking up with Aaron, how February
heat ripens squash and melons, melts glaciers
on the Poles. It's December and we mulch
the garden, cultivate the soil, set in bulbs.
*This fragile earth*, she says.

# NARRAGANSETT BAY

The bay breeze cools but oh it's hot
there in the wood cabin, and the one-holer
smells of Pinesol, dung, and age.
                              I am nine.

Back in my city stale air hangs in corners
still as spiders playing dead.

                              At the beach
two older sisters wait for me each day
their halter tops hold ripening breasts,
I wear my trunks. I'm a mirror to their past
and to my own,

> *the glassy-surfaced sea*
> *a swim too far, the trick-riptide*
> *I couldn't see pulling pigtails,*
> *ribbons —a piercing call,*
> *a human chain, the boy, my mother, dad,*
> *wading, treading through the razor rocks,*
> *arms & poles & sticks reaching me,*
> *shin-bones staining crimson…*

We three girls lie at water's edge, warm,
skin-shriveled, waiting for low tide when quahogs
dive and disappear down wet sand,
leave traces, a mystery of descent.

> *…my fingers search for edges,*
> *I peek into a mirror with one eye,*
> *flirt with the eye, see myself at*
> *sixteen, a worry line between my eyes,*
> *a pimple on my nose…my shadow moves*
> *when I am still, a kind of magic trick*
> *the way that sugar, peaches, cream,*
> *set in a mash of salt & ice, churn & churn*
> *liquid into thick ice cream*

> *it seems for hours*

Mother and I pump, pump,
prime the icy water from deepdown,
beg it into buckets to be heated
on the wood-burning stove. Water hot
for oatmeal or for coffee or

one night each week
for the great galvanized tub set
on a scrubbed wood floor
where this skinny girl of nine slips into her bath,
washes off the salt and sand, slides into bed,

discovers bits of beach between the sheets
and tiny grains in crevices
of pleasure I never knew I had.

**VECTORS**


It is in memory,
our train speeding west

our suitcases packed, heavy with smiles
grinding out miles.

Mother must have   New York to St. Louis
                        from daddy to grandma
mother must have    some months to recover
                        home from the hospital
her room will be dark just like the last time,

our voices low, quiet and crayon
inside the lines, it's expected.

(Daddy, you do belong here)

Just two in the Pullman car, mother and me
                        cigarette ash-air
blue-white around us, a comfort of sorts.




Now it is our turn,
leaving and left again,
money is short, the train trip is long
miles but no motion.

(Empty,
my two chairs, empty, my table, my room and my window,
the glass bowl and barren rock, *Fertile,* my turtle
                        waiting for me.)

                        Cities and stations   successive stops
                        last Tuesday      today      tomorrow *Altoona*

City next city next singing conductor
*South Bend, Terre Haute,*
his diction, so Other, so   so   un-New York.

Snapshots of blue hung on a clothesline,
flash-frozen denim    workpants and aprons,
rusted roofs bleeding  (snap)  darkened like scabs,
alfalfa-green on squares of black earth.

Look at the father plowing for dinner,
my daddy draws at his desk for ours.

※

Beds that the porter pulls out from the overhead,
at nine every night. Sweet sheets
like sun and air, smooth under prickly wool,
curtains of olive cloth snap shut, enclose
me in my house, my own private sun
to switch on and off, under me clip-a-clip, metal on metal.

We saw the engineer once in his cab,
overalls black and white, stripes thin as pencil lines, reading
the semaphores, reading *green-red.*

but  *are we there yet?* We never are.

※

Wind-icy interludes blow through the vestibules,
stretches of warm in between.

White damask tablecloths, glass gleaming silverware,
the sparkle the dazzle, the stacked flannel pancakes
high thick and dark, floating in syrup pools

which tastes just right, here in the dining car.
At last the dining car.

*Fate is a vector,* Andrew will say
many years later, *no state of being,*
*rather, becoming, defining direction.*

Under me clip-a-clip    metal on metal on metal.

## ST. LOUIS SUITE

**i.**

The zoo,
the terracotta walkways,
churning to keep up
with lanky-legged
Uncle Cecil Brin,
tobacco, bourbon, mixed
on his breath,
the scratch of one day's beard.

The dung-wet smell
around the camels' moat,
stronger than
my Bronx zoo's
where you inhale
City all around.

Houses of magic,
green and arid rock,
sand habitats, the aviary's
great domed mesh
high as the hornbill
flies    to perch on
skinny arms of skinny
trees heavy with
rubber leaves,
umbrella-canopies
holding the loamy scent,
droplets, in the air.
You can taste them.

In New York
I fly too, out
the classroom window
facing Central Park
past closed-in rooms
past the dreaded
chalkboard where
I stand and stand

alone,

trying to figure
what plus what
makes nine
exactly

exactly
why I fly above
the Children's Zoo
near 59<sup>th</sup>,

Emma!

back to the classroom
back to the hard chair

back,
my hand in
Uncle's giant paw
the way
a spider monkey
child holds
her mother's hand.
The arc I make
pumping on a swing
not quite as high and wide
as her heart-stopping
swoops, tail to limb
to hand.

St. Louis, Uncle CB's coat,
rawhide, soft with scuffs,
his easy gait
so loose and free,
the way he and his Chevy
move as one,
the leather driving gloves
that hold their shape,

without his hands,
as he lights up a cigarette,
whistles through the smoke.

Our friends in common
and our enemies:
my mother (his sister)
too exacting for us both,
and Aunt Ida's
never-smile-thin-lips,

*Don't mind her, she's a sourpuss,
he'd say,* of  his  own  wife!

but I can't even think
such thoughts —except right here,
except with him.

My leap, at least as wide
as spider monkeys, hand
to heart, my drop
more dangerous,
sharing this truth,
CB and I,
bearing equal weight
in secret and in trust,
as grownups do.

**ii.**

*Teakettle teakettle*
*tea tea tea*

MisterWren
wings in sticks,

tufts and sticks
one by one.

Let him rest,
their nest is done.

❁

The nest's undone!
She's tossing tufts, flinging twigs

as he watches
from a bough, warbles full

*Teakettle teakettle*
*tea tea tea*   even though

the nest's unsprung,
even though

she plucks new tufts, tucks
cottonwood fluff

with her beak,
her thin grim beak.

Even so Uncle whistles
every day

*Teakettle teakettle*
*tea tea tea*

**iii.**

Mrs. Krieg's house
rises from the street
like a behemoth frowning,
brownstone face mounting
four, five stories to slit-eyed
windows that watch
you from the street.

You have to know
the rules here
because Mrs. Krieg
accompanied Rudolph Serkin,
four hands, two pianos
and so
she knows how to do
everything

the right way

which is why
you have to sit
only here
on the strait-backed
side chair,
not there,
on the tufted flowered one
with mauve flocking

where her daughter,
the one
with the lobotomy, sat
and wet her pants
and Mrs. Krieg had to
reupholster,

which is why you don't
interrupt
someone older
and why only Auntie Ida,
her other daughter,
can pour the water
from a crystal pitcher

into goblets just up
to a certain level that
Mrs. Krieg says I can't see
which is why I can't pour,

but I can see, more than the water level,
and Uncle Cecil Brin knows I can.

**iv.**

I wonder every time I climb the stairs
to Mrs. Krieg's,
will I be allowed?

Dark house,
the stink of polish
properly in place like
her tables and chairs.
She talks mean
if you are not just right
and I am not.
She talks mean if you are.

At the zoo I saw a peacock
strutting his stuff, fanning
his iridescent, show-off tail,
his gravel-squawk flayed
my skin.

Up the carved staircase
past the suite Mrs. K shares
with tiny Mr. K, a gentle man,
up another flight
to CB and Auntie Ida's books
and ashtrays, soft-scuffed leather
furniture just like his jacket
only stuffed. You have to be careful
what you say, Mrs. K listens, even here.

She is everywhere
except in Uncle's cellar shop
where the incandescent bulb
swings low, yellow circles spill
back    forth    back,
flooding CB's woodwork bench,

every saw
and size of awl,
a lathe or two,
the smell of glue
for pasting,
posters, plywood
joined as one
waiting for the jigsaw.

We swoop with jungle toucans,
spoonbills, trumpeters, flying egrets,
chatter with the nightjars,
frogmouths, whippoorwills.
Zoo-birds streak our aviary
orange   rust   green.

Up the stairs
we lay our puzzle whole
on Auntie Ida's and CB's table,
jumble it, work to fit the shapes, find
the peacock's ragged iridescent tail,
the reptilian face set
in the frogmouth's head,
make the picture whole.

Upstairs nothing works,
the puzzle pieces won't fit.

**v.**

*See-yeeer, see-yeeer*

her razor-screech—stop!
outsiders both of us.
She eyes me, flares
her plumage double-size,
spreading feet, red tail, wings
wide. Fearsome

hooded beak, hooded
hawk eyes search
the aviary, feathers
cold-gray-white,
flat against her skull,
head like winter.

*See-yeeer, see-yeeer*

**vi.**

Grandmother Julia's cooking eggs in her Pullman kitchen,
*soft-cooked, for my darling*, she says, words from crevices
inside her tidy heart — so private, so open, her slender frame,
long neck inclined over eggs spooned from their shells
as though (years later I would call it courting), as though
in some natural act. But I am six and this is spongy ground.
Here's a woman: voice and body as if naked.
Unadorned. In the act of loving. I, who only know
to skip a stone on Great Pond, to belly flop downhill
on my sled. Julia cracks the shells, delicately scoops
the eggs, yolks unbroken, into the paper-thin
Haviland cup flowered pink and green, presents it
to Granddaddy. An offering from her porcelain hands.
His birthright. I have seen him smile a kingly smile for this.

**vii.**

Wild white,
staccato black

Julia's bobolink stacks hyperbolas
in the air over tallgrass prairie,

flashes melody mid-flight,
something like granddad's

light love talk, his dashing
eyes, dark, sharp, the smooth

song, the pipesmoke circles
he blew in her eyes

until they bedded in the grass
—and always the bobolink's

clink-clink, his metallic chirp
in sedge, in cattail,

his molt and skulk in marsh.
She did the wash, hung up sheets,

waited the terrible wait—
*Will he migrate south?*

No more on quiver-wing
singing, wooing in red clover.

He was like that once.

**viii.**

*Sit on Granddaddy's lap.* I am two times six years,
another Midwest visit convening blood and marriage
in one crowded room. And I oblige, my long legs
swing easily, no need to climb up any more.
Around me dull-gray chatter: Hattie, Auntie Ida and CB,
Julia, Mother. Granddaddy's hands, warm and firm,
circle my waist. The chatter hums. Slowly the hands move up,
my colt-legs stiffen, swing fast off his lap.
No one has seen. Everyone has seen. Has anyone seen?
Opaque voices: *Sit on Granddaddy's lap.* I do not move.
Auntie Ida stands apart, Ida of the never-smile-thin-lips,
Ida who I know doesn't like me, Auntie says
firm and loud: *She's too old for that, leave her be,*
and they listen.

**ix.**

One by one I assemble in my eyes the lives I know:
Here's Julia on her knees scrubbing the kitchen floor
calling to Granddaddy,
                    *Darling, the sky's gone black.*

In 1912 she taught Thackeray in college,
today her love sips Chivas Regal neat at some bar.
One by one I assemble in my eyes lives.

I know Mother scrubs, sews tiny stitches, smocks dresses
for my dolls, spreads silence into each folded frock.
I listen, try to assemble the fractured clothes.

A woman lives in the alley behind my house,
her belongings in a shopping cart carefully arranged
                                        one by one.
We assemble lives, listen to the high wind scrub the sky,
hear low rumblers circle black around
dead calm. The center swollen. Knuckles on a rag.
Julia calls, *The floor is dry now.*

Don't you hear the sound the hoe makes? Espriu asks,
breaking sweet mulch. Uncle CB, Mother, Julia.
One by one I assemble in my eyes the lives I know
as clods break. I call to anyone who'll hear me.

*Coda*

Tonight I dine alone — but "dine" is meant
for damask napkins, crystal, silver spent
on elegance. A kitchen such as mine
holds worn out tools. A fork with crooked tines
tonight blends yolks and whites
into a simple omelet turned just right,
the bottom lightly browned, a half-moon top,
the center creamy, soft as a snowdrop.
The kitchen table from our honeymoon
is set tonight with Julia's sloping spoon,
lopsided, worn by years of scraping pans,
a paring knife that fits close in my hand
and cuts through apple skin like soft butter.
Tonight I'll spoon that omelet for my supper.

# NOTES

page 9
PECHE MERLE
Peche Merle, a cave near Cahors, France with prehistoric drawings
and stenciled hands drawn and printed on white calcite 20,000
years ago.

page 10
WATERVILLE, MAINE, NEAR GREAT POND
The Brazilian Poet Carlos Drummond de Andrade ends his post-
World War I poem, *Souvenir of the Ancient World*, with these prescient
words: *They had gardens, they had mornings in those days!*

page 11
THE CORE BALANCE TRAINER
The Core Muscle Balance Board Trainer: Portions taken from the
Hammacher Schlemmer catalog, Spring 2007.

page 12
SIDEWINDER
The Desert Sidewinder has a dark cheek-stripe on both sides of the
head that starts at the eye and runs diagonally down and backwards
above the mouthline. The snake moves across loose sand with a
sidewinding motion, leaving a series of J marks where it has traveled.

lines 17 and 18, from James Wright's poem *Moon, (Above the River: the
Complete Poems* by James Wright, Farrar, Straus & Giroux, New York,
1992), page 181 … *And I will give you/ My life, my own* …

page 13
A JEW IN THE CUPBOARD
Inspired by Tadeusz Rozewicz's famous poem, *In the Middle of Life*.
In addition to his theme of Poland's rebirth following successive
occupations, Rozewicz talks of nature: bread and water, life in its
many guises, and above all the human condition. *Postwar Polish Poetry*,
edited by Czeslaw Milosz (University of California Press, 1983).

page 17
JENIN, PALESTINE, APRIL 2002
Taken from accounts of the Israeli military incursion into Jenin
on the 14th of April, 2002. (Rick Bragg; The New York Times;
April 15, 2002).

page 29
WEATHER
The poem here is composed of three bouts-rimes. In bouts-rimes,
an old French parlor game, players are given end rhymes and must
compose a verse, usually a sonnet, using them in the order given—
the more peculiar the end rhymes, the greater the challenge.

*The Listener* and *The Reader*, two impassive characters in Samuel
Becket's *Ohio Impromptu*.

page 31
SISTER WENDY AT THE KIMBELL
Centos taken from *Art-loving Nun is Moved by Early Christian Exhibit*
(Gaile Robinson, Fort Worth Star-Telegram, December 2007).
The exhibit, *Picturing the Bible: the Earliest Christian Art*, was held
at the Kimbell Art Museum in Fort Worth, Texas. The complete
quotes from Sister Wendy follow:

(The Good Shepherd) *Early Christians loved the Good Shepherd.
They were an endangered people and protection mattered. Here you have this
beautiful, strong, young Jesus caressing that sheep that he has lifted onto his
shoulders, and all the other sheep are waiting for their turn to be lifted up.*

*We forget that at the beginning people didn't have the certainties that we
have. There wasn't a church in the sense that we have it. The scriptures
weren't settled yet. There was no creed. I found this more touching than I
can find words to express.*

(St. Paul) *Oh you darling man. He's so small and plain with a big nose.
But all this is so unimportant. What is filling his heart is so moving.*

*It begins with the semi-shadows of the catacombs and the scared little people,
and the show ends with this sunburst, full of daylight. It also
suggests the power struggles and dangers of the days ahead.*

page 34
THE DREAM
*I don't love you as if you were salt-rose or topaz,* from Pablo Neruda's
100 Love Sonnets *(Cien Sonetos de Amor,* University of Texas Press,
Austin, 1986).

page 56
VECTORS
The complete definition: VECTOR, a series of consecutive loca-
tions in memory (math); a quantity having direction and magnitude
(math); a carrier of disease; a course steered by a pilot; a carrier,
traveler, rider (Oxford English Dictionary, Clarendon Press,
Oxford, 1993).


pages 59
ST. LOUIS SUITE
part ii (Wren)
*Stalking Birds with Color Camera* (National Geographic Society,
Washington, DC, 1951), p. 36.
*American Bird Biographies* (Comstock Publishing Co., Ithaca, New
York, 1934), pp. 27 – 35.
*A Field Guide to Western Birds* (Houghton Mifflin Company, Boston,
1941), pp. 133 – 135.


part v (Red-tail Hawk)
Weidensaul, Scott, *Raptors, The Birds of Prey* (Lyons and Burford,
New York, 1996), pp. 101, 151, 287 – 289.


part vii (Bobolink)
Chu, Miyoko, *Songbird Journeys, Four Seasons in the Lives of Migratory
Birds* (Walker and Company, New York, 2006) pp.136 –139, 164,
220.


part ix,
The first line of part IX from *Song of Evening's Arrival*, by the great
Catalan poet Salvadore Espriu. (*Selected Poems of Salvador Espriu*,
trans. Magda Bogin, Norton, 1989). Part IX (my poem) was titled
and published as a villanelle, *On a Line from Salvador Espriu.* The
first line of Espriu's poem:

>   *Una a una
>   en els meus ulls ordeno
>   les vides conegides.*

Translated from the Catalan: *"One by one I assemble in my eyes
the lives I know."*

**TEBOT BACH**
A 501 (c) (3) Literary Arts Education Non Profit

**THE TEBOT BACH MISSION:** advancing literacy, strengthening community, and transforming life experiences with the power of poetry through readings, workshops, and publications.

**THE TEBOT BACH PROGRAMS**

1. A poetry reading and writing workshop series for venues such as homeless shelters, battered women's shelters, nursing homes, senior citizen daycare centers, Veterans organizations, hospitals, AIDS hospices, correctional facilities which serve under-represented populations. Participating poets include: John Balaban, Brendan Constantine, Megan Doherty, Richard Jones, Dorianne Laux, M.L. Leibler, Laurence Lieberman, Carol Moldaw, Patricia Smith, Arthur Sze, Carine Topal, Cecilia Woloch.

2. A poetry reading and writing workshop series for the community Southern California at large, and for schools K-University. The workshops feature local, national, and inte national teaching poets. Participating poets include: David St. John, Charles Webb, Wanda Coleman, Amy Gerstler, Patricia Smith, Holly Prado, Dorothy Barresi, W.D. Ehrhart, Tom Lux, Rebecca Seiferle, Suzanne Lummis, Michael Datcher, B.H. Fairchild, Cecilia Woloch, Chris Abani, Laurel Ann Bogen, Sam Hamill, David Lehman, Christopher Buckley, Mark Doty.

3. A publishing component to give local and national poets a venue for publishing and distribution.

Grateful acknowledgement is given to all of our supporters, the Tebot Bach board of directors, Steven R. and Lera B. Smith, and to Golden West College in Huntington Beach, California, all of whom make our programs possible.

Tebot Bach
Box 7887
Huntington Beach, CA  92615-7887
714-968-0905
**www.tebotbach.org**

*This book is set in 11.5 pt Cochin*